Poodle

Series "Fun Facts on Dogs for Kids"

Written by Michelle Hawkins

Poodle

Series "Fun Facts on Dogs for Kids"

By: Michelle Hawkins

Version 1.1 ~January 2021

Published by Michelle Hawkins at KDP

Poodles are very intelligent dogs.

Poodles are great at learning tricks.

Poodles can have many different haircuts.

There are three different sizes of Poodles.

Standard Poodle is fifteen inches or more.

Miniature Poodle is between ten and fifteen inches.

Teacup Poodle is under ten inches long.

Poodles have fluffy hair.

Adult Poodles can sleep up to thirteen hours per day.

The oldest toy Poodle on record was twenty years old.

Poodles are very active dogs.

Poodles can learn over three hundred different words.

Poodles are fabulous at swimming.

The Poodles mouth is very soft and can pick up wounded animals gently.

Poodles fur is naturally curly.

Poodles enjoy people over other dogs.

The more you talk to your Poodle, the more they will understand.

Poodles are fabulous at adjusting to different living arrangements.

Poodles can be trained to ignore gunfire.

The name Poodle means Puddle.

Poodles have very few health issues.

Poodles originally came from Germany.

Poodles are great in hot and cold climates.

Poodles love being in the outdoors to be able to smell everything.

Poodles are considered a very loyal dog.

Poodles will chase small animals.

Poodles are a non-sporting breed of dogs.

Poodles need to be groomed regularly.

Poodles do well at pet-friendly stores.

Toy Poodles are better with teenagers than small children.

The Standard Poodle life span is between twelve and fourteen years.

Poodles shed minimal fur.

Poodles have been used in the military.

Joy is a must in a Poodle's life.

Poodles fur never stops growing.

Poodles can live ten to eighteen years.

Poodles are very sensitive to their surroundings.

Poodles have excellent skills to retrieve water items.

Poodles are aware of their appearance and always enjoy looking good.

The word Poodle, in German, means to splash about.

Poodles have a great temperament

Poodles can be mischievous.

Poodles can sniff out truffle mushrooms.

Poodles need humans to help entertain them; Poodles do not entertain themselves.

A television left on will provide stimulation for your Poodle.

Poodles are great at hunting items.

Poodles are easy to train.

Poodles are considered athletic.

The word Poodle in French means Duck Dog.

Poodles are mostly odorless.

Poodles love to be the center of attention.

Poodles are friendly, from children to older adults.

Poodles need to be brushed daily.

Poodles have a sense of humor.

Poodles have long, hanging ears.

Solid color Poodles can be apricot, black, brown, cream, gray, red, sable, silver, or white.

Make sure that you are always stimulating your Poodle's mind by keeping them thinking.

Poodles have a joy of living.

Poodles need to be professional groomed at least every three to six weeks.

Most Poodles are hypoallergenic.

The best way to train a Poodle is with repetition, patience, and rewards.

Poodles are very graceful dogs.

Poodles can put on too much weight if they are given too many treats.

Poodles were used as war dogs in WW II.

Poodles have a very muscular and sturdy body.

Poodles need you to be talked to firmly but never harshly.

Poodles are very friendly.

The Poodle is the National Dog of France.

Playing hide and seek with toys will keep your Poodles mind stimulated.

Poodles face and eyes need to be cleaned daily.

Poodles enjoy always learning new things.

Poodles have been on the coin of both Ancient Greek and Ancient Romans.

Poodles can be used as guide dogs for people with visual impairment.

Find me on Amazon at:

https://amzn.to/3oqoXoG

and on Facebook at:

https://bit.ly/3ovFJ5V

Other Books by Michelle Hawkins

Series

Fun Facts on Birds for Kids.

Fun Fact on Fruits and Vegetables

Fun Facts on Small Animals

Fun Facts on Dogs for Kids.

Made in the USA
Monee, IL
04 December 2022

19324985R00021